You Started Your Business, Now WHAT???

Accounting Strategies for Small Businesses

Dedication

I want to dedicate this book to my husband, Edwin Ezell, whom I love dearly. My children, Annika, Edwin, and Alexis, along with my grandchildren, MarQuarius, Carsen Hudson, and Aquarius, are all the loves of my life. I am happy to be a wife, mom, and grandma. I want you to know the possibilities are endless. Reach for the stars. To all my mentors and coaches that GOD sent straight from heaven, I want to say Thank You. GOD allowed you to see in me that which I couldn't see in myself. I am genuinely grateful and humbled to know you. Thank you for pushing me to my next.

I love the story of Joseph in the bible, and this scripture stands out to me: GOD not only interpreted what was about to happen but was also given the solution to the problem. May the Josephs arise and bring strategic outlooks to businesses ready to expand.

Genesis 41:33-36: "So now let Pharaoh [prepare ahead and] look for a man discerning and clear-headed and wise, and set him [in charge] over the land of Egypt [as governor under Pharaoh]. Let Pharaoh take action to appoint overseers and officials over the land and set aside one-fifth [of the produce] of the [entire] land of Egypt in the seven years of abundance. Let them gather [as a tax] all [of the fifth of] the food of these good years that are coming and store up grain under the direction and authority of Pharaoh and let them guard the food [in fortified granaries] in the cities. That food shall be put [in storage] as a reserve for the land against the seven years of famine and hunger which will occur in the land of Egypt so that the land (people) will not be ravaged during the famine."

https://my.bible.com/bible/1588/GEN.41.33-36

Contents

Introduction

First, congratulations on starting your business. It's an exciting time, and there is so much to learn. Accounting/bookkeeping is usually a subject most business owners think they already know or are scared to touch. I want this book to inform you and remove the fear from the accounting side of running your business. Nothing is as complicated as we think. Bookkeeping is simple; it takes discipline and order. These are the most critical points in running a successful business.

It is so easy to allow everything to get out of control. Sometimes, we are so worried about getting through the day-to-day that we tell ourselves, "I will look at my finances tomorrow." Then tomorrow becomes tax season. Your accountant or tax preparer must charge extra to put all your paperwork in order. Believe it or not, discipline and order will save you money.

To view your financial situation accurately, keeping a detailed record of all business transactions is essential. Accurate accounting records are crucial for your business's financial health and success. These fundamental principles are discussed throughout this book to help you maintain proper accounting records and needs.

Accrual vs. Cash Basis Accounting: Follow the accrual basis of accounting, which recognizes revenue and expenses when earned or incurred, regardless of when cash is exchanged. This provides a more accurate representation of your business's financial position. The cash basis of accounting, which most small businesses use, accounts for money and expenses when it comes in.

Software and Automation: Utilize accounting software or cloud-based solutions to streamline your record-keeping process. These tools can automate specific tasks, minimize book errors, and provide real-time financial insights.

Chart of Accounts: Set up a well-organized chart of accounts specific to your business. This serves as a framework for categorizing and recording financial transactions. It should include assets, liabilities, equity, revenue, and expenses.

Separation of Business and Personal Finances: Maintain separate bank accounts and credit cards for your business and personal finances. This separation ensures clarity and avoids confusion, making it easier to track and record business transactions accurately.

Documentation: Keep detailed and organized documentation for all financial transactions, such as invoices, receipts, bank statements, and purchase orders. This provides evidence and support for your records and simplifies the auditing process. Establish a record retention policy and adhere to it. Retain your financial documents, such as tax returns, financial statements, and supporting documentation, for the required period as per legal and regulatory requirements.

Bank Reconciliation: Reconcile your bank accounts regularly. Compare your recorded transactions with your bank statements to identify discrepancies and ensure that all transactions are accurately recorded. Timely Recording: Record transactions promptly. Periodically update your books daily or weekly to ensure accuracy and prevent errors or omissions.

Regular Financial Analysis: Perform routine financial analysis and review to assess the health and performance of your business. Compare actual results to budgets and forecasts, identify trends, and make informed decisions based on the information recorded in your accounting records.

It's always a good idea to consult a professional accountant or bookkeeper to ensure your accounting records are accurate, compliant with regulations, and aligned with best practices for your industry and business needs.

Let's Dive In!!

Chapter 1

Cash vs Accrual Accounting

Cash Basis Accounting:

Cash basis accounting is a method of recording transactions based on the actual inflow and outflow of cash. Under this method, revenue is recognized when cash is received, and expenses are recognized when money is paid. It focuses on the cash movements rather than the timing of when payments are earned or costs are incurred. Cash basis accounting is relatively simple and easy to understand, making it suitable for small businesses with straightforward financial transactions. However, it may not accurately represent a company's financial health and performance since it does not consider future obligations or income earned but not yet received.

Accrual Basis Accounting:

Accrual basis accounting records transactions based on when they are incurred, regardless of when the cash is received or paid. It recognizes revenue when it is earned, irrespective of when the payment is received, and recognizes expenses when they are incurred, regardless of when they are paid. This method provides a more accurate picture of a company's financial position and performance by matching revenues with the expenses incurred to generate them. It is commonly used by larger businesses and is required for companies that follow Generally Accepted Accounting Principles (GAAP).

Key Differences:

Timing: Revenue and expense recognition timing is the primary difference between cash and accrual accounting. Cash basis accounting focuses on actual cash inflows and outflows, while accrual basis accounting recognizes revenues and expenses when earned or incurred, regardless of cash movements.

Financial Statements: Cash-based accounting typically results in more straightforward financial statements since it only reflects actual cash transactions. Accrual basis accounting provides a more comprehensive view of a company's financial position and performance by incorporating revenues and expenses earned or incurred but not necessarily received or paid.

Accuracy: Accrual accounting is generally considered more accurate since it matches revenues with the expenses incurred to generate them, providing a clearer picture of a company's profitability. On the other hand, cash accounting may not accurately reflect a company's financial health and performance since it does not consider non-cash transactions and future obligations.

Compliance: Accrual accounting is often required for businesses that follow GAAP or prepare financial statements for external stakeholders such as investors, lenders, or regulatory authorities. Cash-based accounting may be sufficient for small companies with no external reporting requirements.

Choosing the Right Method:

The choice between cash and accrual accounting depends on numerous factors, such as the size and nature of your business, legal requirements, industry norms, and reporting needs. Small companies with straightforward transactions and no external reporting obligations may opt for cash-based accounting due to its simplicity. However, larger businesses or those that need to comply with GAAP generally use accrual accounting for more accurate financial reporting.

It's essential to consult with an accounting professional or financial advisor to assess your specific needs and determine the most suitable accounting method for your business. They can provide guidance based on your circumstances, industry practices, and regulatory requirements.

In conclusion, cash and accrual accounting are two distinct methods with different implications for financial reporting. Understanding their differences and considering the specific needs of your business will help you make an informed decision regarding which approach to adopt.

Take the time to think about whether the cash or accrual accounting method would work better for your business. Jot down the pros and cons for your industry.

_____
_____
_____
_____
_____
_____
_____
_____
_____
_____
_____
_____
_____
_____
_____
_____
_____
_____
_____
_____
_____
_____
_____
_____
_____
_____

Chapter 2

Accounting Software

Accounting software can help you automate your bookkeeping tasks and streamline financial reporting. Useful accounting software is vital in modern businesses, regardless of size or industry. It provides numerous benefits that can significantly impact a company's financial management and overall success. I will discuss some reasons why accounting software is essential to business.

Automation provides accurate and efficient financial management. Accounting software automates various financial tasks, such as bookkeeping, invoicing, payroll processing, and tax calculations. It reduces book errors associated with data entry and calculations, ensuring accuracy and efficiency in financial management. This saves time and resources, allowing businesses to focus on core activities.

Accounting software allows real-time financial insights. Businesses can access up-to-date economic data and generate real-time reports. This enables timely decision-making based on accurate financial information. Managers can monitor cash flow, track expenses, analyze profitability, and make informed business strategies to optimize financial performance.

Streamlined record-keeping makes it easier for all departments. Accounting software simplifies the process of recording and organizing financial transactions. It maintains a centralized database where all financial data, including sales, purchases, expenses, and payments, are stored securely. This streamlined record-keeping ensures data integrity and simplifies auditing and compliance procedures.

Enhanced financial analysis warrants accurate reports. Advanced accounting software provides powerful reporting and analysis tools. It enables businesses to quickly generate various financial statements, such as balance sheets, income, and cash flow statements. These reports offer valuable insights into the company's financial health, aiding in budgeting, forecasting, and identifying trends, strengths, and areas for improvement.

Accounting software improves collaboration and accessibility. Cloud-based accounting software allows multiple users to access and collaborate on financial data simultaneously, irrespective of their geographical location. This facilitates better teamwork and coordination among accountants, managers, and other participants. Additionally, cloud-based solutions offer the advantage of data accessibility from any device with an internet connection.

It offers simplified tax compliance for your business. Accounting software facilitates tax-related processes, such as calculating taxes, generating tax forms, and tracking deductible expenses. It ensures compliance with tax regulations and minimizes the risk of errors or penalties. Some software even integrates with tax filing systems, making tax preparation and filing more efficient.

Automation also allows scalability and integration for holistic processes in your accounting department and business. Useful accounting software can accommodate the changing needs of a growing business. It allows for easy expansion, enabling enterprises to add new features, modules, or users as required. Additionally, integration capabilities with other business systems, such as CRM or inventory management, streamline data flow and eliminate book data entry.

In summary, helpful accounting software provides accurate financial management, real-time insights, streamlined record-keeping, enhanced analysis, improved collaboration, simplified tax compliance, and scalability. By leveraging these benefits, businesses can optimize their financial processes, make informed decisions, and achieve long-term success.

Take the time to think about what accounting software would make your life easier and what it will do for you. Then, research different programs.

_____
_____
_____
_____
_____
_____
_____
_____
_____
_____
_____
_____
_____
_____
_____
_____
_____
_____
_____
_____
_____
_____
_____

Chapter 3

Setting Up Your Chart of Accounts

A chart of accounts helps you track the various types of financial transactions that occur within your business. Having an accurate diagram of funds is essential for reasonably managing the financial records of your business. A chart of accounts is an organized listing of all the accounts used in an organization's general ledger. It provides a framework for organizing and categorizing financial transactions to ensure consistency, accuracy, and ease of reporting.

I have addressed some key benefits of having an accurate chart of accounts below.

Financial reporting relies heavily on the chart of accounts for your business. A well-structured chart of accounts allows for accurate and meaningful financial reporting. It enables you to generate financial statements such as balance sheets, income statements, and cash flow statements that clearly show your business's financial health.

With an accurate chart of accounts, you can easily track and analyze specific reports and categories, enabling informed decision-making. It helps you identify areas of profitability, cost drivers, and financial trends, allowing you to make data-driven business decisions.

Compiling the chart of accounts helps with compliance and tax filings. An adequately maintained chart of accounts ensures compliance with accounting standards and tax regulations. It helps accurately capture and categorize financial transactions, simplifying the process of preparing financial statements and tax returns.

A well-designed chart of accounts can adapt to your business's growth and changing needs. It allows for adding new financial records or modifying existing ones to accommodate new products, services, or business lines.

An accurate chart of accounts promotes consistency and efficiency in recording and reporting financial transactions. It provides a standardized structure for organizing and classifying accounts, making it easier for multiple users to understand and interpret financial information.

To develop an accurate chart of accounts, consider the following guidelines:

Think about the exact things that your business does. Gain a thorough understanding of your business's operations, revenue streams, expenses, and key financial drivers. This knowledge will help you design a chart of accounts that reflects your business's specific needs and goals.

Categorize your accounts into logical groups that align with your business's structure and financial reporting requirements. Common categories include assets, liabilities, equity, revenue, cost of goods sold, operating expenses, and non-operating income and expenses.

Create a hierarchical structure for your chart of accounts, starting with broad categories and progressively breaking them down into more specific subcategories and individual performances. This structure facilitates easy navigation and reporting.

Have a numbering system that is easy for you to remember. Assign unique account numbers to each account in your chart of accounts. Consider using a numbering system that reflects the hierarchical structure and allows easy identification and sorting.

Regularly review and refine your chart of accounts to ensure it remains relevant and aligned with your business's evolving needs. Adjust as necessary to accommodate changes in your business operations or reporting requirements.

Remember, the specific accounts and categories in your chart of accounts will depend on your business type, industry, and reporting needs. Consulting with an accounting professional can provide valuable guidance in developing an accurate and tailored chart of accounts for your business.

Think about how your business runs and the expenses associated with your business. Write them down. If you don't have an automation system, write them down so you will have them.

_____

_____

_____

_____

_____

_____

_____

_____

_____

_____

_____

_____

_____

_____

_____

_____

_____

_____

_____

_____

_____

Chapter 4
Separation of Personal & Business Transactions

This is one of the most important chapters of this book. If processed correctly, it will save you time and a headache. Separating your personal and business finances is necessary to avoid confusion and ensure accurate financial reporting. Separating business and personal finances is essential in running a business for several reasons.

Instituting a clear separation between personal and business finances helps protect your assets from potential business-related liabilities. Keeping your finances separate can prevent creditors or legal entities from going after your assets if your business encounters legal issues, such as lawsuits or debt.

Keeping separate accounts allows for better financial organization and clarity. It simplifies bookkeeping and accounting processes, making tracking business income, expenses, and profits easier. This separation is essential for accurate financial reporting, tax compliance, and obtaining financing for investors.

Separating personal and business finances is crucial for tax purposes. Mixing personal and business transactions can lead to complications during tax filing. Having separate accounts and records lets you quickly identify and report business-related income and expenses, maximizing tax deductions and avoiding potential audits or penalties.

Separating business and personal finances adds to the professionalism and credibility of your business. It demonstrates that you have a well-organized and legitimate operation, which can be critical when dealing with clients, suppliers, and partners. It also helps build trust with financial organizations, making accessing business loans or credit lines easier.

Separating personal and business finances allows you to make better-informed decisions regarding your business's financial health and growth. It enables you to accurately assess your business's profitability, identify improvement areas, and allocate resources effectively. This separation clarifies your business's financial performance and allows you to plan for future investments, expansion, or diversification.

Maintaining a clear separation between personal and business finances is crucial for legal protection, financial organization, tax compliance, professionalism, and strategic decision-making. It is a fundamental practice that helps ensure your business's long-term success and sustainability.

Consider the steps you need to take to separate your personal and business expenses. Write them down.

_____

_____

_____

_____

_____

_____

_____

_____

_____

_____

_____

_____

_____

_____

_____

_____

_____

_____

_____

_____

_____

_____

_____

_____

Chapter 5

Documentation is a Key Component of Your Business's Financial Health

As a small business owner, documenting various aspects of your business is critical for several reasons. Always maintain organized and secure documentation, whether in physical or digital form. Regularly review and update your records to ensure accuracy and importance. You can effectively manage and grow your small business by recognizing the importance of documentation and implementing good practices. When receipts and payments come together, they build your financial outlook. Your reports are more accurate. You will have a clear and concise balance sheet and income statement to track the growth of your business.

Accurate documentation helps ensure that your business sticks to legal requirements and regulations. By keeping records of licenses, permits, contracts, and other legal documents, you can demonstrate compliance with applicable laws, protecting your business from potential legal issues.

Maintaining accurate financial records is essential for managing your business finances effectively. Documenting income, expenses, invoices, receipts, and tax-related information enables you to accurately track cash flow, prepare financial statements, and file taxes. It also helps during audits or when seeking financing from lenders.

Documentation provides a valuable reference for making informed decisions. By documenting past experiences, strategies, and outcomes, you can evaluate what worked well and what didn't. This historical data can guide future decision-making processes, helping you identify patterns, trends, and areas for improvement.

Your paperwork concerning business processes, workflows, and standard operating procedures (SOPs) allows you to streamline operations and enhance efficiency. Clear instructions and guidelines enable employees to perform tasks consistently, reducing errors and ensuring quality. Documentation also facilitates employee training and onboarding, as new hires can refer to documented procedures to understand their roles and responsibilities.

Clear & concise knowledge base records are vital in sharing information within your business. As a small business owner, you may have valuable insights, expertise, and best practices that must be communicated to employees or successors. Capturing this knowledge in written or digital form ensures continuity, even if key personnel leave the company or retire.

By documenting risks, safety procedures, and contingency plans, you can minimize potential risks and ensure the safety of your employees, customers, and assets. This includes maintaining safety training records, incident reports, and emergency protocols. Documentation helps you identify and mitigate potential risks, protecting your business from liabilities and maintaining a safe work environment.

Intellectual property, such as trademarks, copyrights, or patents, safeguards your business's intangible assets. Proper documentation establishes ownership rights and can be instrumental in legal disputes or seeking intellectual property protection.

Documentation is essential when seeking funding, partnerships, or scaling your business. Potential investors, lenders, or partners often require detailed information about your business, such as financial statements, business plans, market research, and growth strategies. Well-documented information boosts your credibility and increases the likelihood of obtaining support for your business growth plans.

Please keep track of all your business receipts to ensure you can claim all your expenses and deduct them to reduce your taxable income. This is something that is missed in most small businesses. These are reasons to keep track of all receipts:

Business receipts serve as evidence of financial transactions and are essential for maintaining accurate financial records. They provide proof of revenue, expenses, and deductions necessary for preparing financial statements, tax returns, and other financial reports.

Receipts play a vital role in tax compliance. They support documentation for business expenses that can be deducted from your taxable income. Without proper permits, you may be unable to substantiate your expenses during an audit, resulting in potential penalties or the disallowance of deductions. In the event of an audit by tax authorities or other regulatory bodies, having well-organized receipts can help demonstrate the legitimacy and accuracy of your financial transactions. It shows that you have maintained proper records and can provide evidence to support your claims, reducing the risk of penalties or further inquiry.

By organizing and categorizing receipts, you can gain insights into your spending patterns, identify areas where you can reduce costs, and make informed financial decisions. This is particularly important for budgeting purposes and controlling expenses.

If you have employees who incur business expenses or if you need to file insurance claims for business-related matters, receipts are essential. They provide documentation for reimbursement processes and support your claims, ensuring you receive the appropriate compensation.

Receipts can serve as proof of purchase, warranties, or contractual agreements. They are valuable in resolving disputes, validating transactions, and protecting your rights and interests as a business owner.

In summary, maintaining a systematic approach to recording and organizing business receipts is essential for accurate record-keeping, tax compliance, expense tracking, audit protection, reimbursement processes, legal obligations, and financial analysis. It helps you stay organized, reduces the risk of errors or penalties, and provides a solid foundation for managing your business effectively.

Keeping track of the payments you receive from customers can make or break a company. It becomes crucial when you don't know how much money you are making and must guess or can't remember what you made because there is no system in place. The importance of keeping track of payments involves the following:

Tracking your payments helps you maintain a clear and organized record of your income. It allows you to quickly identify and analyze your sources of revenue, helping you understand your financial health and make informed decisions.

You can accurately assess your cash flow and budget by keeping track of your payments. You'll better understand when revenues are expected, enabling you to plan for expenses, savings, and investments. This information is precious for individuals, small businesses, and freelancers who rely on a regular income.

Tracking your payments is essential for accurate tax reporting and compliance. It helps you identify taxable income, deductible expenses, and potential tax liabilities. You can use payment records to substantiate your financial transactions and meet your tax obligations.

Occasionally, discrepancies or disputes may arise regarding payments. If you have a clear record of all transactions, you can quickly resolve any issues by referring to your payment history. This record serves as evidence and can help settle client, customer, or financial institution disputes.

In the event of a financial audit, whether it's an internal review or by a tax authority, having a well-maintained payment record is crucial. It demonstrates your financial transparency, supports the accuracy of your financial statements, and simplifies the audit process.

Keeping track of payments conveys professionalism and reliability to your clients, customers, and business partners. It shows that you take your financial matters seriously, which can enhance your reputation and build trust with stakeholders.

Payment records provide valuable data for financial analysis. By analyzing your payment history, you can identify patterns, trends, and opportunities for growth. You can assess the profitability of different products or services, evaluate customer payment behavior, and make informed decisions based on data-driven insights.

Consider using accounting software, spreadsheets, or dedicated payment-tracking tools to track payments effectively. These tools can automate the process, reduce errors, and provide additional functionalities such as generating reports and reminders.

This was a lot, but record-keeping will help keep things together.

Think of some processes to help you keep up with your essential records, receipts, and payments. Write them down.

_____

_____

_____

_____

_____

_____

_____

_____

_____

_____

_____

_____

_____

_____

_____

_____

_____

_____

_____

_____

_____

_____

_____

Chapter 6

Reconciliation of Accounts

Reconciliation of your accounts regularly to identify any discrepancies between your books and your bank balances is essential. Reconciliation of accounts in business refers to the process of comparing and matching the ratios of two related financial records to ensure they agree. This process is typically performed regularly, such as monthly or quarterly, and is crucial for maintaining accurate financial records and identifying discrepancies or errors.

The most common type of account reconciliation is bank reconciliation, where a business compares its internal records of cash transactions with the bank statement. This process helps identify differences between the two and allows for correcting errors or detecting fraudulent activities.

The general steps involved in reconciling accounts include obtaining the necessary records. Gather the relevant financial documents, such as bank statements, the public ledger, cash receipts, and disbursement records.

Start by comparing the opening balances of the accounts in question. For example, if reconciling a bank account, compare the opening balance of your internal records with the opening balance shown on the bank statement.

Review each transaction individually, comparing the entries in your internal records with the corresponding entries on the bank statement. Mark off each transaction that appears in both forms and make note of any discrepancies or missing items.

For any discrepancies found, investigate the reasons behind them. Common causes include timing differences, errors in recording transactions, bank fees, interest income or expenses, and outstanding checks or deposits.

Once you have identified the discrepancies, make the necessary adjustments to your internal records. This may involve correcting errors, recording missing transactions, or updating balances accordingly.

After adjusting, review the reconciled accounts again to ensure all differences have been resolved. Double-check that the ending balances of the reconciled accounts match.

Maintain proper documentation of the reconciliation process, including the date, the accounts involved, the reconciling items, and the adjustments made. This documentation serves as a record for future reference and audit purposes.

By regularly reconciling accounts, businesses can identify errors, prevent fraud, and maintain accurate financial records. It is a necessary practice for financial control and ensures the integrity and trustworthiness of a company's financial statements.

How often do you reconcile your finances? How can you make a habit of reconciling your business accounts?

_____

_____

_____

_____

_____

_____

_____

_____

_____

_____

_____

_____

_____

_____

_____

_____

_____

_____

_____

_____

_____

_____

_____

_____

_____

Chapter 7

Monitor Your Cash Flow

Monitoring your cash flow to ensure you have enough funds to cover your expenses is essential. Monitoring business cash flow is a vital aspect of managing a thriving business. Cash flow refers to the movement of money in and out of your business, including revenue from sales, expenses, and investments. By monitoring cash flow, you can understand your business's financial health and make informed decisions to improve its performance. We will discuss steps to monitor your business cash flow successfully.

Record every transaction in your business, including sales, payments received, bills, operating expenses, loan repayments, and other financial activities. Use accounting software or spreadsheets to keep accurate and up-to-date records.

Develop cash flow projections or predictions that estimate your expected inflows and outflows over a specific period, typically monthly or quarterly. This will help you anticipate potential cash shortages or surpluses.

Keep track of outstanding customer payments and follow up on any overdue invoices. Implement efficient invoicing and collection processes to ensure timely payments from your customers.

Stay on top of your payables and manage your vendor relationships effectively. Negotiate favorable payment terms and avoid late payment penalties. Take advantage of early payment discounts whenever possible.

Regularly review your cash flow statements, summarizing your cash inflows and outflows during a specific period. Analyzing these statements will help you identify patterns, trends, and potential areas for improvement.

Pay attention to any negative or low cash flow periods. Identify the underlying causes, such as seasonal fluctuations, late customer payments, unnecessary expenses, or unsuccessful inventory management. Take corrective actions to address these issues promptly.

Build a cash reserve or emergency fund to cover sudden expenses or cash flow gaps. This will provide a safety net during tough times and ensure your business can operate smoothly.

Look for strategies to improve your cash flow, such as negotiating better payment terms with suppliers, reducing unnecessary expenses, pursuing additional revenue streams, or optimizing inventory management.

If you find it challenging to manage your business's cash flow effectively, always consider consulting with an accountant or financial advisor. They can provide valuable insights, help you implement best practices, and offer guidance on cash flow management.

Remember, consistent monitoring and proactive management of your business cash flow are essential for maintaining financial stability and supporting long-term growth.

Because most businesses have cash-based accounting, monitoring cash flow is hard. Think about a process that will help you monitor your cash flow so that you don't end up with more months than money.

_____

_____

_____

_____

_____

_____

_____

_____

_____

_____

_____

_____

_____

_____

_____

_____

_____

_____

_____

_____

_____

_____

_____

Chapter 8

Using Financial Reports

Financial reports can provide you with valuable awareness of the financial health of your business, helping you make informed decisions. Accurate financial statements are vital for businesses as they offer a detailed and transparent view of the company's financial performance and position. These reports help stakeholders, such as investors, lenders, and management, make informed decisions about the business. Some of these topics may sound repetitive, but this is how they all unite. These fundamental elements and facts for using accurate financial reports in the industry will help clarify what was already discussed.

Follow the accounting standards and principles outlined by your country's important governing bodies or accounting standards boards. GAAP (Generally Accepted Accounting Principles) provides guidelines for recording, classifying, and presenting financial information.

As a small business owner, we should understand the financial reports connected to our business. They provide insights into your company's profitability, cash flow, and financial stability. Here are some essential financial statements that small business owners should know.

Income Statement (Profit and Loss Statement)

This report summarizes your business's revenues, expenses, and net profit or loss over a specific period, usually monthly, quarterly, or annually. It shows how much money you made and spent during that period.

Balance Sheet

The balance sheet provides a snapshot of your business's financial position at a specific time, typically at the end of a month, quarter, or year. It lists your assets (what you own), liabilities (what you owe), and equity (the net worth of your business).

Cash Flow Statement

This report tracks the cash flow in and out of your business over a specific period. It shows how changes in your income, expenses, accounts receivable, and accounts payable impact your cash balance. Monitoring cash flow is critical for managing day-to-day operations and ensuring you have enough cash to cover expenses.

Statement of Changes in Equity

This report outlines the changes in your business's equity over a specific period, typically a year. It includes contributions by owners, net income or loss, distributions to owners, and other adjustments that impact the equity accounts.

Accounts Receivable Aging Report

This report helps track outstanding customer invoices and their aging if you sell products or services on credit. It categorizes receivables by their due time, allowing you to identify potential collection issues or bad debts.

Accounts Payable Aging Report

This report tracks and categorizes your outstanding vendor invoices based on their unpaid time. It helps you manage your cash flow by ensuring timely vendor payment and avoiding late fees.

Budget vs. Actual Report

This report compares your actual financial results with the budgeted amounts. It helps you identify variances between projected and actual performance and enables you to adjust your business operations or budget as necessary.

It's important to note that different businesses may have unique reporting requirements based on industry, size, and legal obligations. Using accounting software or online tools can simplify generating and analyzing financial reports. Ensure that all financial transactions are recorded accurately and promptly. This includes capturing all revenue, expenses, assets, and liabilities in the appropriate accounts. Regularly reconcile accounts to identify and rectify any discrepancies. Implement robust internal controls to safeguard assets, prevent fraud, and ensure accuracy. This may involve segregation of duties, regular reviews, approvals, and checks and balances to minimize errors and irregularities in financial reporting.

Apply consistent accounting policies and methods across financial periods to ensure comparability. Changes in accounting policies should be disclosed and explained in the financial reports. Regularly reconcile financial statements with supporting documentation, such as bank statements, invoices, and receipts. Perform thorough reviews of financial information to identify and correct any errors or inconsistencies.

Employ qualified and experienced accounting professionals with the knowledge and expertise to prepare accurate financial reports. Stay updated with the latest accounting standards and regulations. Engage external auditors to conduct independent reviews of financial statements. External audits provide an additional layer of assurance and help identify any material misstatements or weaknesses in internal controls.

Provide clear and comprehensive disclosures in financial reports. Include footnotes, management discussions, and analysis to explain significant accounting policies, estimates, and other relevant information. Leverage accounting software and financial management systems to streamline processes, reduce errors, and improve accuracy. Automation can help with data entry, calculations, and reconciliation.

Provide ongoing training and professional development opportunities for the finance and accounting team to enhance their skills and knowledge. This ensures they stay updated with best practices and accounting standards.

By following these practices, businesses can enhance the accuracy and reliability of their financial reports, encouraging confidence in stakeholders and facilitating informed decision-making. Consulting with an accountant or financial advisor can help determine which reports are most relevant to your business needs.

What could you accomplish with accurate financial reports? How would you run your business if you knew how much your business is worth?

_____

_____

_____

_____

_____

_____

_____

_____

_____

_____

_____

_____

_____

_____

_____

_____

_____

_____

_____

_____

_____

_____

_____

_____

Chapter 9

Consult a Professional

Consider consulting a professional bookkeeper or accountant to ensure your bookkeeping is accurate and current. When looking for an accountant, consider the following steps:

Determine Your Needs: Define the specific accounting services you require. This could include tax preparation, bookkeeping, financial analysis, or other specialized services.

Seek Recommendations: Ask friends, family, or business associates for referrals. Personal recommendations can be valuable in finding a reputable and reliable accountant.

Research Qualifications: Look for certified accountants and members of professional accounting bodies, such as certified public accountants (CPAs) or chartered accountants (CAs). These designations indicate that the accountant has met specific educational and professional requirements.

Verify Experience: Consider an accountant who has experience working with clients in your industry or with similar financial situations. They will likely be more familiar with the challenges and regulations specific to your business or personal finances.

Interview Potential Accountants: Schedule consultations with a few accountants to discuss your needs and assess their expertise and compatibility. Ask about their experience, services, fees, and communication practices during the interview.

Check References and Reviews: Request references from the accountant and follow up with past or current clients to understand their satisfaction with the accountant's services. Additionally, check online reviews and ratings.

Consider Fees: Inquire about the accountant's fee structure. Some accountants charge an hourly rate, while others may offer fixed fees for specific services. Make sure you understand the costs and how they will be determined.

Communication: Clear and effective communication is crucial when working with an accountant. Ensure that the accountant is responsive and able to explain financial concepts and strategies in a way you can understand.

Remember, the accountant-client relationship is a partnership, so finding an accountant you feel comfortable working with and who has your best interests in mind is essential.

When do you think you should contact an accountant? How could an accountant expand your business?

_____
_____
_____
_____
_____
_____
_____
_____
_____
_____
_____
_____
_____
_____
_____
_____
_____
_____
_____
_____
_____
_____
_____
_____
_____

Chapter 10

Some Businesses Need a Strategist.

An accounting strategist is responsible for developing and implementing financial strategies and initiatives within an organization. Their role involves analyzing financial data, identifying areas for improvement, and providing recommendations to optimize financial performance.

Contact an accounting strategist to elevate your business.

A strategist conducts in-depth financial analysis to assess the current economic state of the organization. This involves reviewing financial statements, analyzing key performance indicators (KPIs), and identifying trends and patterns. Based on the financial analysis, an accounting strategist develops strategic plans to enhance the organization's financial position. They work closely with senior management to set financial goals, identify growth opportunities, and establish strategies to achieve them.

Cost management is a critical function of an accounting strategist. They assess the organization's cost structure, identify cost-saving opportunities, and develop strategies to reduce expenses without compromising quality or efficiency. Accounting strategists play a vital role in the budgeting and forecasting process. They collaborate with various departments to develop accurate financial forecasts and budgets that align with the organization's strategic objectives. They also examine actual financial performance against the budget and provide variance analysis.

They assess financial risks and develop strategies to mitigate them. They identify potential financial threats, such as market volatility, regulatory changes, or operational risks, and develop risk management plans to safeguard the organization's financial stability. An accounting strategist establishes performance metrics and key indicators to evaluate the organization's economic performance. They develop reporting frameworks and dashboards to monitor financial results, track progress toward goals, and provide regular performance updates to management.

Accounting strategists identify inefficiencies and holdups in financial processes and systems. They collaborate with cross-functional teams to streamline processes, execute automation tools, and improve the accuracy and effectiveness of financial operations. They ensure compliance with accounting standards, regulations, and internal policies. They stay updated with changes in accounting regulations and assess their impact on the organization. They also establish internal controls and governance frameworks to preserve financial integrity.

They communicate financial knowledge and insights to various stakeholders, including senior management, board members, investors, and external auditors. They prepare financial reports, presentations, and recommendations to facilitate decision-making and provide guidance on financial matters.

An accounting strategist mixes financial expertise with strategic thinking to drive economic growth, improve resources, and boost the organization's financial health. Contact an Accounting Strategist to elevate your business.

Think of ways an accounting strategist could help you grow your business. How could your business capitalize if you had the strategy to excel and expand? Is a strategist for you, or do you need a bookkeeper at this point in your business?

_____

_____

_____

_____

_____

_____

_____

_____

_____

_____

_____

_____

_____

_____

_____

_____

_____

_____

_____

_____

_____

_____

_____

_____

Conclusion

I wrote this book to inform business owners on accounting skills vital for their business's growth. This may seem minor to some, but just these few tools can take you to new heights. Accounting strategies can make or break a business, and I want to help. Education is critical when you can't afford an accountant or strategist. Knowing the difference between accrual and cash accounting for your books will allow you to understand how to account for your money. Correctly choosing your software and setting up a chart of accounts will help you run your business efficiently and effortlessly. Once your systems are set up, tracking receipts and payments will be easy. We must know where our money is as small business owners. Cash flow is essential because if we don't know what we have, making necessary purchases or decisions is hard to make us profitable. It is vital to reconcile our bank accounts as business owners to have accurate financial reports to know where our business stands as an institution. All these processes work together to keep the finances of our companies together.

Making notes after every chapter and thinking about your next moves will help if you consult a professional and allow you to have more understanding of the conversation you will have for advisory. This will work, even if you are considering an accountant, to bring strategy to your business and move to bigger goals. We start businesses to grow, which is my hope for everyone who reads this book.

If you are at a point in your business where the next level is upon you, reach out to an accountant business strategist to partner with you. Partnership is critical in the next phase of your business.

NOW GO FORTH AND DO GREAT THINGS!!!!

Author's Bio

Keesha Ezell, a seasoned professional in the field of accounting with over two decades of experience, is a distinguished graduate of Liberty University, where she earned a prestigious degree in Accounting. Additionally, she holds a Business Administration degree from John Tyler, showcasing their well-rounded expertise in both financial and business administrative domains.

Throughout her illustrious career, Keesha Ezell has demonstrated an unwavering commitment to excellence and a passion for delivering top-notch financial solutions. Keesha's profound knowledge and practical experience have enabled her to establish KG Tax and Accounting Solutions, a thriving enterprise dedicated to providing comprehensive financial services to businesses and individuals alike.

As the founder and driving force behind KG Tax and Accounting Solutions, Keesha has been instrumental in helping numerous clients navigate the complexities of financial management with unparalleled skill and dedication. Her remarkable journey, from academic accomplishments to entrepreneurial success, serves as an inspiration to aspiring professionals and entrepreneurs in the accounting and business administration fields.

In her latest book, You Started your Business, NOW WHAT? Keesha shares invaluable insights gleaned from her extensive experience, offering readers a wealth of practical advice and strategic guidance for achieving financial success. Drawing from real-world examples and a deep understanding of the intricacies of accounting and business administration, Keesha provides a compelling roadmap for individuals and businesses seeking to optimize their financial strategies and achieve sustainable growth.

Through her writing, Keesha continues to shape the future of accounting and business administration, leaving an indelible mark on the industry and inspiring others to pursue excellence in their financial endeavors.